EDGE BOOKS™

Agricultural DRONES

by Simon Rose

Consultant:
Todd Golly
Chief Operating Officer/Founder
Leading Edge Technologies

CAPSTONE PRESS
a capstone imprint

Edge Books are published by Capstone Press,
1710 Roe Crest Drive, North Mankato, Minnesota 56003
www.mycapstone.com

Library of Congress Cataloging-in-Publication Data
Names: Rose, Simon, 1961- author.
Title: Agricultural drones / by Simon Rose.
Description: North Mankato, Minnesota : Capstone Press, [2017] | Series: Edge books. Drones. | Includes bibliographical references and index. | Audience: Age 8-14. | Audience: Grade 4 to 6.
Identifiers: LCCN 2016023851| ISBN 9781515737674 (library binding) | ISBN 9781515737759 (pbk.) | ISBN 9781515737957 (ebook (pdf)
Subjects: LCSH: Aeronautics in agriculture--Juvenile literature. | Drone aircraft--Juvenile literature. | Agriculture--Remote sensing--Juvenile literature.
Classification: LCC S494.5.A3 R67 2017 | DDC 631.3--dc23
LC record available at https://lccn.loc.gov/2016023851

Editorial Credits

Carrie Sheely, editor; Steve Mead, designer; Tracey Engel, media researcher;
Katy LaVigne, production specialist

Photo Credits

Alamy: © 67photo, Front and Back Cover, blickwinkel, 11, Chris Biele, 12–13; AP Images: Ng Han Guan, 24; Getty Images: Kathryn Scott Osler/The Denver Post, 15, Bloomberg/Michael Nagle, 19; iStockphoto: Onfokus, 8–9; Newscom: Mike De Sisti/TNS, 20–21; Shutterstock: Alexander Kolomietz, 28–29, Andis Rea, Design Element, Brothers Good, Cover and Interior Design Element, DamienGeso, Design Element, Eric Isselee, 16, Fotokostic, Cover Background, Kolonko, Design Element, Konstantin Ustinov, Design Element, Nik Merkulov, Cover and Interior Design Element, Mykola Mazuryk, Cover Background, Olivier Le Moal, 18, Pagina, Design Element, PointImages, 4–5, robuart, Design Element, Steve Collender, 6–7, TMsara, 10, Vjom, Cover and Interior Design Element; The Image Works: Kike Calvo/V&W, 23, 26; USGS, 17

TABLE OF CONTENTS

CHAPTER 1

Solving a Mystery

A puzzled and worried farmer looks out over his field. He has a problem with his crops. Some of the plants are wilting and others are growing more slowly than they should. His fields are very large. He doesn't have time to walk through his fields and check the plants. The farmer isn't sure what is causing the problem. The plants could be growing in poor soil or have inadequate access to water. Diseases or pests could also be causing the problem. The farmer wants more information before deciding what to do.

Luckily, he has exactly what he needs in his barn. It is a small drone with rotors.

FACT

Drones that fly are also called unmanned aerial vehicles (UAVs).

The farmer enters a flight path for the drone using his smartphone. He programs in the area of the field where the drone should take photographs and video. The drone flies on its own, but the farmer watches as it crisscrosses the field. After about 20 minutes, the drone returns to the farmer and lands. The farmer **downloads** the data from the drone to his laptop computer.

FACT

Some drones can cover 200 acres (81 hectares) in about 20 minutes.

The farmer examines the images the drone's camera has captured. He zooms in on some images and sees evidence of pests on the leaves. He also notices dry patches in the soil where the plants lack water. The farmer now knows what he needs to do to manage his crops.

download—to move or copy data from an electronic device or website to another electronic device

CHAPTER 2

Eyes in the Sky

Agricultural drones have a lot in common with other UAVs. Like most other drones, agricultural drones are equipped with cameras, sensors, and **navigation systems**. But there are some differences. Agricultural drones are usually smaller than military drones or commercial drones used by businesses. They also carry less equipment and do not spend as much time in the air. Agricultural drones have the most in common with recreational drones that people fly for fun.

Agricultural drones are some of the most affordable drones. Advanced recreational drones might cost up to $5,000. Military drones may cost millions of dollars. A basic agricultural drone may cost less than $1,000.

FACT

In the United States most crops are on farms that have at least 1,100 acres (445 hectares).

A man inspects his onion crop with a Typhoon Q500+ drone.

Many Uses

Drones can be helpful to both crop and livestock farmers. Crop farmers use agricultural drones to **survey** fields and sections of crops. Companies that provide crop surveying services to farmers also use these drones. Livestock farmers use drones to monitor the health of animals and track their movements.

navigation system—equipment that allows a vehicle to follow a course from one place to another

survey—to look over and study closely

Advantages of Agricultural Drones

Why use a drone? The advantages are numerous. Farmers and ranchers often have very large properties. It can be difficult to travel long distances to manage animals or crops. Drones can save travel time and expenses by checking a farmer's property more efficiently. Drones can track animals' movements. They can check crops for signs of disease and pests. They can gather information on the number of plants and their heights. They also can show growing conditions, such as soil moisture. Some drones can even spray herbicides or pesticides to help crops grow. Herbicides kill weeds, and pesticides kill insects and other animals that can damage plants.

plant showing signs of disease

An agricultural drone's camera is its most useful feature. These cameras take high-**resolution** images that have very clear detail. These photographs are less expensive to get than those taken by **satellites** or manned aircraft such as helicopters. Agricultural drones fly very low, so their cameras are unaffected by cloud cover.

resolution—describes a device's ability to show an image clearly and with a lot of detail; low-resolution images don't show as much detail as high-resolution images

satellite—a spacecraft used to send signals and information from one place to another

AERIAL TREE SURVEYS

The high-tech cameras on agricultural drones can be useful for other jobs. In 2012 on the Kintyre peninsula in Scotland, a fungus called *Phytophthora ramorum* had spread from rhododendrons to larch trees. Thousands of trees had to be cut down to try to stop the fungus from spreading further. Forest managers there had a great idea. They decided to use drones to monitor the situation.

Drones took photographs of the forest's remote areas. Their cameras took close and detailed images of the trees and their leaves. These images helped forestry managers see when a tree was in the early stages of disease. The tree could then be cut down before the disease spread to other trees nearby.

The Kintyre peninsula is heavily forested.

Flying by the Rules

People who fly any type of drone need to follow rules. Countries make their own rules about drone use, although not all countries have drone laws. In the United States, the Federal Aviation Administration (FAA) sets rules for drone use. The FAA currently limits drone flights to a height below 400 feet (122 meters). The operator must be able to see the drone at all times. Drone flights are not allowed within 5 miles (8 kilometers) of airports without permission.

According to FAA rules, drones must operate in daylight. They can operate during twilight only if the drone has anticollision lights.

In 2016 the FAA changed it rules for drones weighing under 55 pounds (25 kilograms) for business purposes such as farming. People no longer need to get a permit for business use of drones. But operators do need to be at least 16 years old, complete certification training, and follow all FAA rules. Those without training may still fly if they are supervised by someone who has completed training.

CHAPTER 3

Drone Parts and Features

Although agricultural drones share some features, the technology in them varies. For example, an operator on the ground can control an agricultural drone with a **remote control**. The operator directs the drone to areas that need to be photographed. Some drones can also fly by themselves on a preset flight path. Farmers must match the drone's technology with their individual needs. The more technology a drone has, the more it usually costs.

Wings and Rotors

Most agricultural drones have either fixed wings or **rotors**. Fixed-wing drones look like small airplanes. They can cover a wider area than rotor drones and fly for longer periods of time. Fixed-wing drones also can carry more equipment and collect more information quickly in one flight. They are usually more expensive than rotor drones. Farmers often use them to take scans that can be used to make a **3-D** image of a field.

remote control—a device used to control machines from a distance

rotor—a set of rotating blades that lifts an aircraft off the ground

3-D—having or appearing to have length, depth, and height

maneuverable—able to move and control easily

A technician assembles a fixed-wing drone at agricultural drone manufacturer Agribotix in Boulder, Colorado.

Rotor drones operate like small helicopters. They use rotors to fly. Multirotor drones have more than two rotors. Drones with four rotors are called quadcopters. Rotor drones are more **maneuverable** than fixed-wing drones. They can hover over certain parts of a field and fly closer to the ground than fixed-wing drones. They also need less room to take off and land.

Cameras

Agricultural drones can carry different types of cameras. **Thermal** cameras detect plant and soil heat. Plants that are **dehydrated** will give off more heat than plants that have enough water intake. Farmers can use this data to create a map of the field that shows areas of increased heat.

Near-infrared cameras can help show plant health and **chlorophyll** levels. Healthy plants reflect near-infrared light differently than unhealthy ones do. When a plant becomes dehydrated or sick, the plant doesn't reflect as much near-infrared light. The healthy plants then show up in a different color on the image than unhealthy plants.

RGB cameras capture images with very accurate colors. This helps farmers assess the health of plants by studying the color of their leaves.

FLYING HERDERS

In 2015 an Irish farmer used a small drone to herd a flock of sheep between different fields. The drone's camera helped the farmer make sure that no animals were lost. The sheep responded to the drone, which may mean that local border collies may one day be out of a job!

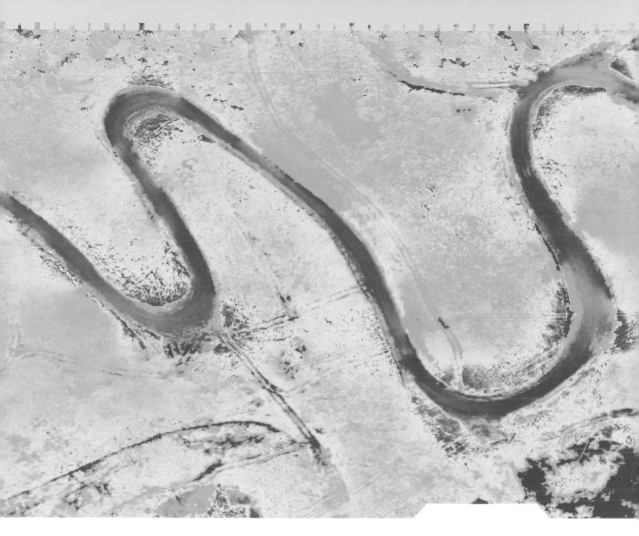

Data from near-infrared cameras can be used to create maps of fields. In this image the red areas show healthy plants. The blue areas show less healthy plants.

thermal—having to do with heat or holding in heat

dehydrated—not having enough water

near-infrared—related to short wavelengths of radiation that are not visible to people

chlorophyll—the green substance in plants that uses light to make food from carbon dioxide and water

Agricultural Drone Sensors

Sensors on drones measure things that are not normally seen. For example, accelerometers sense movement or vibrations and keep a drone stable when it is flying. Some drones are equipped with thermal sensors that can detect an animal's temperature. This helps a farmer know if any livestock have a fever. Some drones can even detect weather conditions such as high winds. High winds can make a preprogrammed flight too difficult for a drone. The drone can then automatically return to base.

FACT

In 2014 the company Stevia First made plans to fly drones with LED lights over stevia crops at night. The leaves of stevia are used to make artificial sweeteners. The LED light helps the plants produce their sweet ingredient more quickly. The company began its flights near Sacramento, California.

Workers assemble a drone at a manufacturer in Brooklyn, New York. Workers carefully assemble drones to be sure the sensors and other parts work properly.

Bodies and Motors

Drone bodies are made from light composite materials such as **carbon fiber**. Composite materials are as strong as metal but weigh much less. These materials are often used in spacecraft and other aircraft. Composite materials reduce a drone's weight and give it more maneuverability.

Agricultural drones have battery-powered electric motors. The type and size of battery determines how long the drone can stay in the air. Most agricultural drones stay in the air less than an hour before needing to be recharged.

FACT

Shake, shake, shake, and fly! To start the motor of the eBee agricultural drone, the operator just shakes it three times. Then the operator simply throws it into the air.

In 2015 British company Intelligent Energy invented a way to extend drone flight times. It added a **hydrogen** fuel cell to the regular battery. By doing this, a small drone was able to fly six times longer. Agricultural drones may use this technology in the future.

A pilot tests an agricultural drone in Mazomanie, Wisconsin.

carbon fiber—a strong, lightweight material made with acrylic fiber using high temperatures

hydrogen—a colorless gas that is lighter than air and burns easily

GPS

Drones are equipped with **Global Positioning System** (GPS) navigation systems. GPS uses a system of satellites orbiting Earth. The satellites work together to pinpoint exact locations on Earth's surface. A GPS receiver communicates with the satellites to tell a drone operator exactly where the drone is on its flight path.

Using GPS, a farmer can plan a drone's route to only fly in a certain area of a field. He or she can set the route so that the drone flies around obstacles. Some drones can be programmed to return to their takeoff locations. The farmer can then pick up the drone after its flight.

FACT

Some researchers are building agricultural drones with robotic arms. These drones could someday pick pests off plants.

Global Positioning System—an electronic tool used to find the location of an object; this system uses signals from satellites

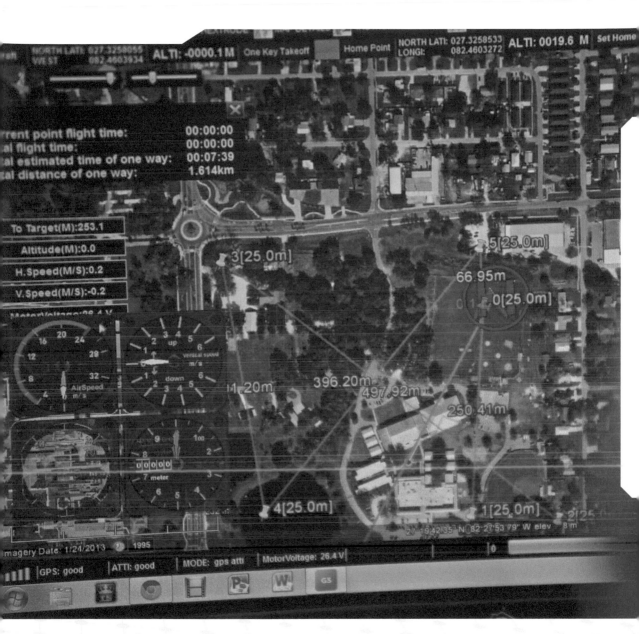

An operator can easily set a preset flight path for a drone by looking at a map on a screen. The operator can then choose places for the drone to fly.

CHAPTER 4

Flying into the Future

Experts believe that drone use will expand around the world in the coming years. Most of these drones will be small machines such as the ones used by farmers. The FAA estimates there will be at least 7 million drones flying in the United States by 2020. Of the drones purchased for business use, more than 80 percent are likely to be used in agriculture. According to the FAA, recreational and commercial drone sales are expected to rise from 2.5 million in 2016 to 7 million in 2020.

An agricultural drone flies over a field in China in 2015. It is demonstrating how drones can be used to spray pesticides.

Reasons Behind Drone Expansion

What are the reasons behind increased drone use? One big reason is the improving technology of drones. Drones are not only becoming smaller but also cheaper. This means that even more farmers will be able to afford them.

For some countries, other factors could contribute to an increase in agricultural drone use. Japan's population is aging, and many of the country's rice farmers are elderly. Fewer young people are interested in working in agriculture. Drones can help fill in for fewer workers. In China the drone industry is booming. The government promotes the use of modern farm machinery, including drones.

FACT

Some farmers think of creative ways to use their drones. In Suffolk, England, a farmer is using his drone to scare away pigeons from his crops. This helps keep the pigeons from eating his crops.

Locals of Nepal, Asia, learn how to fly a drone during a humanitarian workshop in 2015.

Feeding the World

The United Nations predicts that Earth's population will be 9.7 billion by 2050. If everyone on the planet is to be fed, improvements need to be made to agriculture. Drones can help check the amount of water in the soil and monitor plant health. In turn, farmers can make the best use of their water resources and use fewer chemicals.

The population is expected to increase the most in developing countries. Better food production in these areas could help sustain the population increases. As drones become less expensive, more farmers in developing countries may be able to buy them. A group of farmers in these areas could buy one drone and share it.

SOME OF THE LEAST DEVELOPED COUNTRIES

The United Nations keeps track of which countries in the world are least developed. Africa currently has the largest number of countries on this list. This chart shows some of the least developed countries as of May 2016.

COUNTRY	GEOGRAPHIC AREA OF WORLD
Burundi	AFRICA
Niger	
Madagascar	
Zambia	
Malawi	
Eritrea	
Nepal	ASIA
Bangladesh	
Afghanistan	
Myanmar	
Solomon Islands	AUSTRALIAN COAST
Haiti	CENTRAL AMERICA

More Drones and New Laws

Governments will likely need new drone laws as more people use them. These laws can help prevent collisions between unmanned aircraft and people, power lines, and other aircraft. Some agricultural drones also carry dangerous chemicals that might hurt people or animals if the drones crash.

More laws could also help protect the privacy of the public. Some people do not want drones with cameras to fly over their private property. Without privacy laws, an operator could use a drone to secretly spy on the property of a neighboring farmer.

Agricultural drones are a huge help to farmers around the world. Laws guiding drone use will help ensure that drone use can continue to expand.

Lawmakers are still exploring privacy laws for drones in the United States. Current FAA laws address safety concerns for drones more than privacy concerns.

GLOSSARY

3-D—having or appearing to have length, depth, and height

carbon fiber (KAHR-buhn FY-buhr)—a stong, lightweight material made with acrylic fiber using high temperatures

chlorophyll (KLOR-uh-fil)—the green substance in plants that uses light to make food from carbon dioxide and water

dehydrated (dee-HY-dray-tuhd)—not having enough water

download (DAUN-lohd)—to move or copy data from an electronic device or website to another electronic device

Global Positioning System (GLOH-buhl puh-ZI-shuh-ning SISS-tuhm)—an electronic tool used to find the location of an object; this system uses signals from satellites

hydrogen (HYE-druh-juhn)—a colorless gas that is lighter than air and burns easily

maneuverable (muh-NOO-ver-uh-buhl)—able to move and control easily

navigation system (NAV-uh-gay-shuhn SISS-tuhm)—equipment that allows a vehicle to follow a course from one place to another

near-infrared (NEER-in-fruh-RED)—related to short wavelengths of radiation that are not visible to people

remote control (ri-MOHT kuhn-TROHL)—a device used to control machines from a distance

resolution (re-zuh-LOO-shun)—describes a device's ability to show an image clearly and with a lot of detail; low-resolution images don't show as much detail as high-resolution images

rotor (ROH-tur)—a set of rotating blades that lifts an aircraft off the ground

satellite (SAT-uh-lite)—a spacecraft used to send signals and information from one place to another

survey (sur-VAY)—to look over and study closely

thermal (THUR-muhl)—having to do with heat or holding in heat

READ MORE

Faust, Daniel. *Commercial Drones. Drones: Eyes in the Skies.* New York: PowerKids Press, 2016.

Marsico, Katie. *Drones.* Engineering Wonders. New York: Children's Press, 2016.

Scholastic. *Drones: From Insect Spy Drones to Bomber Drones.* New York: Scholastic, 2014.

INTERNET SITES

FactHound offers a safe, fun way to find Internet sites related to this book. All of the sites on FactHound have been researched by our staff.
Here's all you do:

Visit *www.facthound.com*

Type in this code: 9781515737674

Check out projects, games and lots more at **www.capstonekids.com**

Capstone Captivate is published by Capstone Press, an imprint of Capstone.
1710 Roe Crest Drive
North Mankato, Minnesota 56003.
www.capstonepub.com

Library of Congress Cataloging-in-Publication Data is available on the Library of Congress website.
ISBN: 978-1-5435-9193-4 (hardcover)
ISBN: 978-1-4966-5783-1 (paperback)
ISBN: 978-1-5435-9200-9 (eBook PDF)

Summary:
Learn all about the surprising facts, amazing stories, and legendary players found in this book.

Image Credits
Associated Press: Brett Coomer, 24, Elaine Thompson, cover, Jim Mone, 5, Kamil Krzaczynski, 29, Kevork Djansezian, 7; Dreamstime: Danny Raustadt, 9, Doug James, 8, 23 (top), Keeton10, 11; Newscom: Icon SMI/SI/John McDonough, 13, 15, 21, Icon SMI/Richard Clement, 16, MCT/Hyosub Shin, 23 (bottom), Reuters/Rebecca Cook, 17, Reuters/Robert Galbraith, 14, TNS/Aaron Lavinsky, 19, USA Today Sports/Brad Rempel, 26, USA Today Sports/Jennifer Buchanan, 10; Shutterstock: EFKS, 1

Design Elements: Shutterstock

Editorial Credits
Editor: Gena Chester; Designer: Sarah Bennett; Media Researcher: Eric Gohl; Production Specialist: Spencer Rosio

Printed and bound in China.
PA99

Table of Contents

Glossary terms are **bold** on first use.

The Big Game Winner

The Los Angeles Sparks played the Minnesota Lynx in the last game of the 2016 WNBA Finals. Most fans thought the Sparks would win. But the game was neck-and-neck. With just 3.1 seconds left on the clock, Sparks forward Nneka Ogwumike grabbed a rebound and tried to shoot. Her shot was blocked, but she grabbed the ball again.

Falling backward, she tossed up one more shot. This time she got nothing but net! The Sparks led 77–76. They held on to win the game and the 2016 WNBA Finals.

Fast Fact!

Minnesota Lynx head coach Cheryl Reeves has the most **playoff** wins of any coach in WNBA history. She's tied for the most WNBA championships with four.

Nneka Ogwumike sinks a shot while falling backwards.
Her basket was the deciding play in the 2016 Finals.

CHAPTER 1

The History

On April 24, 1996, the board of directors for the National Basketball Association (NBA) voted to create a women's pro basketball **league**. The new league would be called the Women's National Basketball Association (WNBA). The WNBA featured eight teams. The first game tipped off in June of 1997. The New York Liberty faced the Los Angeles Sparks.

That game drew in 14,284 fans. The Liberty defeated the Sparks by a score of 67–57. The regular season was underway. Each team played 28 games.

The Originals

The WNBA started with only eight teams, split into two **conferences**. The Eastern Conference had the Charlotte Sting, Cleveland Rockers, Houston Comets, and New York Liberty. The Los Angeles Sparks, Phoenix Mercury, Sacramento Monarchs, and Utah Starzz made up the Western Conference.

L.A. Sparks center Zheng Haixia (middle) shoots over Rebecca Lobo of the New York Liberty.

Once the regular season was complete, the playoffs started. The four teams with the best records competed against each other. After a first round of playoff games, only two teams were left. The Houston Comets beat the New York Liberty in a one-game Finals Championship. It was the start of many wins for the Houston Comets.

Detroit Shock player Katie Smith calls out a play during a regular season game. In 2009, the Shock eventually moved to Dallas, Texas, and are now called the Dallas Wings.

Lynx star Maya Moore attempts a shot. The Mercury went on to win the game and the Western Conference Finals 85–71 in 2014.

Over one million fans went to see WNBA games that first season. The new league was considered a success. It was ready for season number two. For the second season, two more teams entered the league—the Detroit Shock and Washington Mystics.

The WNBA has continued to grow and change. Today, there are 12 teams in the WNBA. They are the Atlanta Dream, Chicago Sky, Connecticut Sun, Indiana Fever, New York Liberty, Washington Mystics, Dallas Wings, Los Angeles Sparks, Las Vegas Aces, Minnesota Lynx, Phoenix Mercury, and Seattle Storm.

Each season, the top four teams from each conference go to the playoffs. There are four rounds of games. In rounds one and two, each team plays just one game. Winning teams move to the next round. Losing teams in the first two rounds are out of the playoffs.

Seattle Storm guard Jewell Lloyd (right) goes for a layup in Game 2 of the 2018 WNBA Finals.

The Dallas Wings pass the ball around the Mercury defense in a 2017 game.

Round three, the Conference Finals, is a best-of-five series. That means the team that wins three games first wins.

The two winning teams from the third round play each other in the WNBA Finals. This is also a best-of-five series. The first team to win three games is named the WNBA Champion for the season.

CHAPTER 2

Great Teams

Houston Comets: 1997–2000

In 1997 through 2000, it looked like the new WNBA league was going to belong to the Houston Comets. Teammates Cynthia Cooper, Cheryl Swoops, and Tina Thompson helped the Comets win the first four WNBA Finals. During those four seasons, the Comets won 114 games and lost only 26. The Comets won every time they reached the WNBA Finals.

The early success of the Houston Comets was not enough to keep the team alive. The team shut down in 2008. A search for new ownership had failed. The Comets were dropped from the WNBA.

The Houston Comets celebrate winning the 2000 WNBA Championship. Cynthia Cooper (14) won the WNBA Championship Most Valuable Player Award for the second time.

Fast Fact!

The Women's Basketball Hall of Fame is in Knoxville, Tennessee. Cynthia Cooper and Tina Thompson were added in 2009 and 2018.

Nikki Teasley of the Sparks and Tari Phillips of the Liberty dive for a loose ball. The Sparks won Game 2 of the 2002 Finals 69–66.

Los Angeles Sparks: 2001–2003

The Los Angeles Sparks picked up where the Comets left off. They play in the Staples Center. That's also where the Los Angeles Lakers play. The Sparks head coach, Michael Cooper, had been a star player for the Lakers.

The Sparks were led by Lisa Leslie. The 6-foot, 5-inch tall center helped them win 28 games in 2001. They lost only four games that season. In the playoffs, they won the Conference Semifinals and WNBA Finals without losing a single game.

In 2002, they did it again. The Sparks won the Championship without losing a single playoff game. In 2003, they made it to the Finals a third time but were defeated by the Detroit Shock.

All-Star player Lisa Leslie shoots a free throw in the 2001 WNBA Finals. Leslie retired from the league in 2009.

Detroit Shock: 2003–2008

The Shock had the WNBA's worst record in 2002. New head coach Bill Laimbeer made big changes to the **roster**. He added Ruth Riley, Cheryl Ford, and Kendra Holland-Corn to the lineup. These players added big talent in scoring and rebounding. From 2003 to 2008, the Detroit Shock were one of the best teams in the WNBA.

In 2003, they defeated the Los Angeles Sparks to win the WNBA Finals. Center Ruth Riley was named the WNBA Finals MVP. They won the Finals again in 2006 and 2008. They made it to the Finals in 2007 but were defeated by the Phoenix Mercury.

The Shock's Swin Cash dribbles up the court during Game 3 of the 2006 WNBA Finals.

Detroit Shock players Plenette Pierson (left) and Cheryl Ford celebrate a made shot by Ford in Game 2 of the 2008 WNBA Finals.

The Shock remained a strong team for several years. They went from one of the WNBA's worst teams to one of the best. A lack of money forced the Shock to move to Tulsa, Oklahoma, in 2010. In 2015, the team moved again. This time they became the Dallas Wings.

Minnesota Lynx: 2011–2017

The Minnesota Lynx entered the WNBA in 1999. It took the team 12 years to make it to the Finals. The 2011 season started one of the strongest WNBA teams ever.

The Lynx won the Finals in 2011 behind the strong play of Seimone Augustus. They weren't done. They won it all in 2013, 2015, and 2017.

WNBA stars like Maya Moore, Sylvia Fowles, and Lindsay Whalen made them a great team year after year. Head coach Cheryl Reeves became the most successful coach in WNBA history.

Fast Fact!
The Lynx and Houston Comets share the record for winning the most WNBA Finals Championships. They each have four.

Lynx guard Seimone Augustus (middle) steals the ball from fallen Sparks forward Nneka Ogwumike. The Lynx have made it to the WNBA Finals six times.

Hardwood Heroes

Cynthia Cooper: Houston Comets

Cynthia Cooper was 34 years old when she played her first WNBA game. Despite her age, she was an immediate star. She led the Houston Comets to four straight WNBA Finals Championships. She was the WNBA Finals MVP each time.

She is the all-time leader in points-per-game in the WNBA. Her average was 21 points-per-game during regular seasons. When it was playoff time, she got even better. After four playoffs, she averaged 23.3 points-per-game.

No one has ever been as consistently good in the playoffs as Cooper. She retired in 2004. Five years later, Cooper was voted into the Women's Basketball Hall of Fame in 2009.

Cynthia Cooper shoots a free throw during Game 2 of the 2000 WNBA Finals. Cooper helped the Comets win several WNBA Championships.

Angel McCoughtry: Atlanta Dream

Angel McCoughtry can do it all. She was the WNBA Rookie of the Year in 2009 and helped Team USA win two gold medals at the Olympics. She's been an All-Star five times. She's a great defender and scorer.

But when the Atlanta Dream go to the playoffs, she really shines. In 2010, McCoughtry set the WNBA record for most points in a playoff game. She scored 42 points in the conference finals game against the New York Liberty. Her team won 105–93.

The next year, she saved her best for Game 2 of the WNBA Finals. She scored 38 points against the Minnesota Lynx. That's the most points by one player ever in a WNBA Finals game.

Fast Fact!

WNBA players usually play **overseas** during their off-season. Playing overseas is a great way for WNBA players to make more money. But without the rest that comes with an off-season, players are more at risk for injury.

Angel McCoughtry (right) drives to the hoop during a game against the Phoenix Mercury.

McCoughtry goes up for a layup in Game 3 of the 2011 WNBA Finals.

Teresa Weatherspoon: New York Liberty

The New York Liberty were facing the Houston Comets in the 1999 WNBA Finals. The Comets held a 2–0 lead in the series. With just 2.4 seconds left to play, the Liberty were trailing by two points. Confetti began to fall onto the court as the Comets fans began to celebrate.

The game wasn't over yet. The Liberty threw a long **inbound pass** in to guard Teresa Weatherspoon. Weatherspoon took two quick dribbles toward the hoop and launched a half-court shot. The ball smacked the backboard and went in for a 3-point shot. The Liberty won the game!

While the Comets won the championship in the next game, Weatherspoon's half-court shot is one of the most memorable moments in WNBA history.

New York Liberty's Teresa Weatherspoon is swarmed by her teammates after making an amazing, buzzer-beating shot from half court. With Weatherspoon's shot, the Liberty took the Comets to a deciding Game 3 in 1999.

Lynx forward Maya Moore dribbles against Sparks defender
Odyssey Sims.

Maya Moore: Minnesota Lynx

Minnesota Lynx star Maya Moore is great at proving herself in big moments. In Game 3 of the 2015 WNBA Finals, she made one of the biggest shots in WNBA history.

With just 1.7 seconds left to play, the game was tied 77–77. Teammate Lindsay Whalen threw an inbound pass in to Moore at the top of the 3-point line. Moore faked a shot, then stepped to her right. The defender flew past her. Moore jumped and fired. The ball went through the net perfectly! The shot gave Minnesota the win by a score of 80–77.

Fast Fact!

Maya Moore is a highly decorated athlete. She has been an All-Star six times and won the All-Star MVP three times. She's scored more points in WNBA All-Star games than any other player.

Diana Taurasi: Phoenix Mercury

Phoenix Mercury guard Diana Taurasi likes the number three. She wears jersey number three. She's even the all-time career leader in 3-pointers in the WNBA.

So it's no surprise that her biggest moment came during Game 3 of the 2014 WNBA Finals. The Mercury were winning the series 2–0. The game was tied with just under 15 seconds left to play when Taurasi took a running shot just outside the lane.

Taurasi made the basket and was also fouled by her defender. She made her free throw to make it a 3-point play. The Mercury won the game and the Finals for their third WNBA Championship.

Equal Pay?

The average WNBA player is paid around $79,000 annually. The league limits **salaries** to at most $117,500. In comparison, the starting salary for men in the NBA in 2019 was $582,180. The salary limit for an NBA player was $109 million for the 2019–2020 season. LeBron James made $35.65 million in 2018. That's enough money to pay the salaries of all players in the WNBA for two full seasons.

Mercury guard Diana Taurasi shoots in Game 3 of the 2014 WNBA Finals. In 2015, Taurasi's overseas team in Russia paid her to sit out of the upcoming WNBA season. The move sparked further debate over paying WNBA players a fair salary.

Glossary

conference (KAHN-fuhr-uhns)—a grouping of sports teams that play against each other

defense (di-FENS)—the team that tries to stop points from being scored

inbound pass (in-BOWND PASS)—a pass from outside the playing area into the playing area

league (LEEG)—a group of sports teams that play against each other

overseas (o-vur-SEES)—in or to a country that is not in North America

playoff (PLAY-awf)—a series of games played after the regular season to decide a championship

roster (ROSS-tur)—a list of players on a team

salary (SAL-uh-ree)—money paid on a regular schedule to people doing a job